7-DAY SUGAR DETOX METHOD:

SUGAR IS THE DEVIL(GUIDE, PLAN AND WORKBOOK)

by HEATHER NEWMAN
www.SugarDetox7.com

WELCOME

If you've found yourself here, reading this book, I'm sure you have been struggling with SUGAR most of your life. Being a complete chocoholic for most of my life, I am fully aware of the addiction. The scary thing is that sugar comes in so many forms, we may think we are eliminating it from our diet when in fact, we are still supporting the addiction through other food sources. I call this the sneaky sugars. They are the ones that most people aren't really clear on or aware of. It's not as cut and dry as the sugar found in candy, cake and cookies. Regardless of your sugar cravings, through whichever avenue you struggle with the most, you are in the right place and I'm so glad we are on this journey together for the next 7-days.I would truly love to hear from you once you've finished my sugar detox plan. Please be sure to subscribe to my website at www.GlitterU.com and leave your testimonial from this journey at www.SugarDetox7.com.

Let's get this party started! Promise me you'll try to stay nice to everyone around you while you cleanse your mind, body and soul from the sugar(s).

Contents

THE TRUTH ABOUT SUGAR

I've always said, "Sugar is the devil". It comes into your life every day disguised as something really sweet and delicious, but it's literally killing us on the inside. I won't make this about the Devil because I refuse to give him the attention he wants...But I will devote our time together talking about SUGAR and the horrible things it is doing to us all.

SUGAR-- it's been a struggle for me most of my life. It doesn't just ruin your nutrition plans and leave a big pocket of fat around your belly but it brings you down and leaves you feeling tired and sluggish every day around 3pm, are you with me?

Scientists declare, and I agree, that sugar is very TOXIC AND ADDICTIVE!

Since I basically define sugar as another type of drug, quitting it isn't easy. The sugar addiction is very real, so we are in this together and we are going to grab this bull by the horns and tackle this beast together! Me and YOU!

This guide is going to help you ditch your sugar cravings for good so you can learn to enjoy it. It's a high highs, low lows kind of thing. That mid day cookie might make you feel great for an hour, but it can leave you exhausted when your body finishes processing the sugar. You feel like you need a pick-me-up, so where do you turn? Well, this is where the cycle begins. You turn to more sugar. It's a vicious cycle that is difficult to break until NOW.

I am going to arm you with a new weapon that is going to give you everything you need to kick the addiction.

I'm going to show you how to avoid it and beat it! You will have all of your SWEET POWER back once and for all! These tools will always be here in your new 7-DAY SUGAR DETOX toolbox so keep this guide by your side, give it to a friend as a sweet gift and share it with others who might need to break up with SUGAR too!

When we talk about sugar, most think about the types of sweets that I mentioned earlier, (the C's) candy, cake and cookies. Well, guess what? I know you don't want to hear this but sugar is in most everything we eat. It's honestly prevalent in most things that we don't even think about unless you started on a clean eating journey and really make a decision to pay close attention (like you will after doing this 7-Day Sugar Detox with me). I'm going to list some items below and I want you to circle the ones that you THINK have added sugars in them:

Yogurt	Pasta sauce	Coleslaw	Bread
Milk	Granola	Juice	Ketchup
Salad dressing	Dried fruit	Marinade	Instant oatmeal
Energy drinks	Packaged fruits	Granola bars	Breakfast cereals

The answer?

You might have guessed it, ALL OF THEM!

Did you get them all correct? All of these have enough sugar to keep the craving alive and thriving. So why do we care? Well, besides the fact that it's linked to major depression and mood swings (which by the way, that's enough to get my full attention and it should be for you as well), sugar can really mess with you mentally. The scary thing about sugar is that it can really wreak havoc on your brain and your body. Scientists link sugar to weight gain (shocker!), a higher risk of heart disease, cancer, acne and of course cavities. I am all too familiar with cavities, sad but true. Sugar causes inflammation and bloat, giving us major joint pain. It can make us age faster and really screw up our pancreas, liver and kidneys. This is why it is so important to break this habit or atleast get it under our control.

Addiction is hard in any capacity so this is not going to be easy but I believe in you, I believe in us and we can do this together! So, grab my hand, this book and a friend, we are going on a 7-day Sugar Detox journey and we will NOT let that DEVIL get us derailed!

- Truth be told is you just don't want to give those foods up or make a change bad enough at this stage of your life. You're pretty sure "later" is a better time for you or you're hoping someone has a secret for you to instantly make them go away.

- #1 It's because of our want for instant gratification. We don't really think long and hard enough about the benefit of delayed gratification and where we could be 24 hours, 7 days, 6 months and 10 years down the road without these unhealthy choices affecting our health.

- #2 We really haven't made the effort to educate ourselves on just how bad these choices are. Like severe disease bad! For those that drink diet soda every day or a Monster energy drink or even Cheetos and a taquito from the gas station… if you really knew how hard and nutrient depriving that was on the body, you would feel more empowered to make better choices for you and the kiddos.

- Big food companies have become magicians at hiding the ugly. If you "saw" what you were eating (minus the bright colors, enticing smell and palette pleasing chemicals) you'd change your mind.

- So it really comes down to owning your decisions and knowing consequences will come or starting to educate yourself now and making small changes that will lead to big ones that will have a profound effect on your quality and quantity of life down the road.

SUGAR DETOX FOOD GUIDE

Where do we find sugar? There are different types of sugar. Key words to know are:

SUCROSE:	Made up of glucose and fructose found in plants. Table sugar.
FRUCTOSE:	This sugar is found in fruit and honey.
GALACTOSE:	Milk and other dairy products contain this sugar.
GLUCOSE:	You can find this sugar in fruit, veggies and honey.
LACTOSE:	Found in milk, made of glucose and galactose.
MALTOSE:	Found in barley.
XYLOSE:	Found in wood or straw.

Enough to make your head spin right? All of the "--ose" words that we have to learn and keep straight makes this SUGAR DETOX sound pretty challenging. On top of seeing the "--ose" words sugar is also hiding under a bunch of other sneaky names. I'm sure you are aware of the high-fructose corn syrup, right? Do you know why we should stay clear of this? Well, the high-fructose corn syrup is just SUGAR SYRUP. There are plenty of names that sugar hides behind. I'll help you here with a list so you can keep an eye on ingredient labels. Keep this little list handy when you head to the grocery store. I told you, SUGAR IS THE DEVIL - hiding everywhere!

OTHER NAMES FOR SUGAR:

Besides beets and cane, sugar also can be derived from honey, many fruits (such as dates and coconuts) and tree saps. Molasses isn't technically a sugar; it's actually potent black syrup that's a byproduct of when sugar is extracted from beets or sugarcane. White sugar contains almost no molasses, but brown or "raw" sugar contains some. Molasses can also make brown sugar stickier and, of course, a darker shade of brown.

Sugar crystals, particularly white sugar, may come in different granulations. Some common types are:

Icing: very small crystals that quickly dissolve in liquids or can be used for decorating desserts, like confectioners' sugar
Caster: larger crystals than icing
Granulated: basic table sugar, with larger crystals than caster or icing
Preserving: very coarse sugar used as a preserve in jams and similar confections

We identify sugar with sweetness, which is one of the four main tastes, along with bitter, sour and salty (and umami). These tastes correspond to particular taste buds on the human tongue. A taste bud activates when a molecule of the appropriate shape touches it, then sending a message to the brain indicating what type of taste it is dealing with.

Besides evoking pleasure, sweetness can indicate that a food is safe to eat. Many naturalists advise nibbling on a tiny portion of a wild plant to determine if it's poisonous or not. A bitter taste indicates that the plant is likely unsafe.

In the human body, glucose is used for cellular respiration. For this reason, it is often referred to as BLOOD SUGAR because it travels through the BLOOD and diffuses across cell membranes. But to get glucose (and fructose), the body must break down sucrose, a task aided by the enzyme sucrase. While sugar essentially powers human cells, it is still basically empty calories. It provides a quick boost of easily processed energy but little else. Sugary foods rarely have any of the other carbohydrates, proteins, vitamins and minerals necessary for a healthy diet. And as you recall, any excess sugar in the body won't be used as energy and will be stored as fat. Yep, probably right in the belly.

Obesity, which excessive sugar consumption certainly can contribute to, boosts the chances of developing type 2 diabetes. Also, high blood-sugar levels cause the body to produce an excess of insulin, potentially damaging the pancreas. It can hinder the passage of block proteins. There are various types of diabetes, and complications from the disease are potentially fatal--another reason why sugar should be consumed in small to moderate quantities.

Finally, mind your teeth: Sugar is the leading cause of cavities. Glycoproteins from sugar stick to the teeth and become magnets for bacteria. The bacteria eat the fructose in sugar and produce lactic acid as a by product. The lactic acid can contribute to the wearing down of tooth enamel and the formation of cavities.

HOW MUCH IS TOO MUCH?

The American Heart Association recommends no more than 6 teaspoons (25 grams) of added sugar a day for women and 9 teaspoons (36 grams) for men. But the average American gets way more: 22 teaspoons a day (88 grams). It's easy to overdo. just one 12 ounce can of regular soda has 10 teaspoons of sugar and zero nutritional benefit.

FOODS TO AVOID:

FRUIT IN MODERATION

Fruit is super healthy and worth working into your diet. That said, fruit is full of sugars. They are natural sugars, but they are still sugar. Keep your fruit consumption down to a couple a day. Make sure you are getting more veggies than fruit to get the nutrients your body requires and you are not loading up on accidental sugar!

GRAINS: A HIDDEN DANGER

I love bread too but when you are trying to cut sugar, it's not your friend, EVER! Some grains already have added sugars, but even if they don't, they definitely have starch. After you eat it, starch converts to sugar in your body. Here is my rule: skip the bread and start with a salad instead.

PACKAGED FOODS: SO MUCH ADDED SUGAR! BEWARE!

Seriously, added sugars are in so much stuff. This actually makes me so sick to my stomach to think that as a consumer we are just not told the truth up front. I've found the easiest way to skip added sugars is to stay clear of packaged foods as much as possible. Low-fat foods, in particular, are so risky since manufacturers use sugar to add flavor. The best advice I can give to keep it as simple and easy to navigate is to always look at the label and stay clear of any of those "--ose" words.

FOODS TO ENJOY! FINALLY!

Ok, the part you've been waiting so patiently for right?! What CAN WE EAT? What is good for us? How do we stay away from all the sugars, and what's that leave us with? Know that this 7-Day Sugar Detox is not just going to be a restrictive bummer to make us all crabby patties! The 7-Day Sugar Detox is designed to make it easier than you could ever imagine to kick the sugar habit and addiction to the curb. It is full of delicious, nourishing foods you can and will really enjoy. I promise!

VEGGIES: AS MUCH AS YOU WANT!

I really can't say enough about how good veggies are for you. I'll be honest, i'm not a huge fan of all veggies but now that I understand we eat for fuel and not for our emotional distress and how sugar works in our systems, I see how right my momma was! So, get to that Farmers' Market and look for vibrant, colorful veggies that you can put into your meals to make them beautiful and nourishing. And the best part is they are SUGAR FREE, so you can eat as much as you wish. My personal favorite is spinach. I'll share some recipes at the end of this book for you to try too!

FATS: THE GOOD KIND!

Yes, my favorite part of this 7-Day Sugar Detox is this part right here. Fat is your friend. Eating healthy fats can help you feel full and keep any of your cravings away. Being hungry is NOT WHAT THIS DETOX is about. Enjoy the healthy fats like avocados, nuts and coconut oil while you avoid sugar.

PROTEIN: THE KEY TO STAYING BALANCED!

Protein, protein, protein! Everyone talks about it like they know exactly what they are doing and how it fuels our bodies, but do you really know? I'm going to suggest trying to put a little bit of protein into every meal, including your breakfast. Adding a little protein (don't over do it though) every time you eat will keep you full longer and keep your blood sugar balanced, making this entire journey a lot easier.

Know that this is just a quick overview. We will dive deeper into the details soon. Are you ready? Ok, great,

Let's go!!

WHAT TO EXPECT WHILE YOU ARE SUGAR DETOXING!

Now that you are cutting out the sugar, you are going to feel very different. In the end, you will feel great, I promise. In the interim, it might be a little rough but I want you to know YOU CAN DO THIS! It's only 7-days. Most of us are addicted to sugar and don't even realize it. Even if you are not a huge candy, cake and cookies lover, sugar might have a bigger hold on you than you even realize.

Have you ever done any type of detoxification before? If you have, then you already know some of the warnings I'm about to give you. You are going to have withdrawal symptoms and yes, they are not going to be fun. You might become a little cranky at times, that's expected. But that's actually how you know it's working! You are cleansing!

Why giving it up can feel lousy;

A number of studies have found that sugar affects the brain the same way that addictive substances such as nicotine, cocaine, and morphine do. With the average American consuming 22 to 30 teaspoons a day — considerably more than the recommended maximum of 6 teaspoons — some withdrawal symptoms are to be expected.

Our brains have a reward system that helps us survive as a species. Food is a natural reward, and consuming something sweet stimulates our brain's reward system.

Though experts are still divided on whether sugar addiction is a real thing, animal and human studies have found that sugar triggers the release of dopamine in the nucleus accumbens — the same area of the brain implicated in response to heroin and cocaine.

Eating sugar regularly changes your brain so that it becomes tolerant to the sugar, causing you to require more to get the same effect.

Sugar has also been shown to cause the release of endogenous opioids in the brain, which leads to a rush similar to that experienced when a person injects heroin. All of this leads to a vicious cycle of cravings and needing more sugar to feel good.

When you cut out sugar, your cravings get more intense and you experience withdrawal symptoms — at least at first.

Sugar detox can cause unpleasant physical and mental symptoms. How the body reacts to quitting sugar is different for everyone. Which symptoms you experience and the severity of these symptoms depend on how much sugar you were consuming.

Withdrawal symptoms can last from a few days to two weeks. The longer your body goes without sugar, the less intense your symptoms and cravings for sugar will be.

You may find that your symptoms are worse at certain times of the day, such as between meals. Stress is also known to trigger cravings for sugar, so you may find your symptoms seem worse during times of stress.

The first couple of weeks might produce the following symptoms:

Headaches: This isn't unlike a caffeine withdrawal. Headaches are common and completely normal.

Energy funk: You know that energy crash you feel after you eat a bunch of candy, cake or cookies (sugar)? That low energy, tired and cranky feeling? Well, rest assured, you are going to be feeling that on a much bigger scale. Keep your head up! This too shall pass, I promise. To me it's the hardest part but the detox is ultimately going to leave you feeling more energized than ever!

Cravings: Shocker right? Not really! When you cut out an addictive substance, you want it more. You are definitely going to have sugar on the brain. In these situations, keep yourself full of water and make sure you are getting plenty of protein and healthy fats. This will help minimize those cravings (DEVIL).

Brain fog: Your brain actually uses sugar as energy, so cutting back can lead to you feeling a little fuzzy and confused. This too shall pass. I myself, keep focussed by drinking my "Unicorn Juice". You can find out more about that on my blog at www.GlitterU.com if you'd like to try it.

Feeling a bit bummed out, grumpy or cranky: When you eat sugar, your brain releases dopamine, the chemical that makes you feel happy. When you are not eating sugar you may notice that you are not getting the same "pick-me-up" feeling from your afternoon snack. The good news is that once you get through this part of the detox, you'll feel better than you have in years. You will feel more energized and more in control of what you want to eat. You'll drop those belly inches, get glowing skin, shiny hair, gain your zest for living again and probably want to exercise a bit more to take care of your overall health. Once you gain control of the sugar addiction, you will notice that anything with sugar in it tastes sweeter and you'll only need a tiny bit of it so you will feel more like you are "treating" yourself (aka the way sugary treats are supposed to be consumed).

MENTAL SYMPTOMS

My 7-Day Sugar Detox can cause a number of emotional and mental symptoms. Let's summarize these here:

Sugar detox can cause a number of emotional and mental symptoms. These include:

- Depression. Feeling down is a common sugar withdrawal symptom. Along with low mood, you may also notice a lack of enjoyment in things you once found pleasurable.

- Anxiety. Feelings of anxiousness may also be accompanied by nervousness, restlessness, and irritability. You may feel like you have less patience than usual and are on edge.

- Changes in sleep patterns. Some people experience changes in their sleep when detoxing from sugar. You might find it hard to fall asleep or stay asleep through the night.

- Cognitive issues. You may find it difficult to concentrate when you quit sugar. This can cause you to forget things and make it hard to focus on tasks, such as work or school.

- Cravings. Along with craving sugar, you may find yourself craving other foods, such as carbohydrates like bread, pasta, and potato chips.

PHYSICAL SYMPTOMS

Headache is one of the most common side effects of sugar detox, along with feeling physically rundown. Other possible physical withdrawal symptoms include:

- light-headedness and dizziness
- nausea
- tingling
- fatigue

Giving up sugar can make you feel lousy, but rest assured, it will get better if you stick to your sugar detox. You can break your sugar addiction in these 7 days.

HERE'S OUR GAME PLAN

Are you ready to get this party started? Turn on the lights, pump up the jam and let's do this thing! I know you are so over sugar running your life and you want to become the healthiest version of yourself so here are the steps you'll need to take. Stick with this guide for at least one week and you'll be able to live your life free from THE DEVIL's sugar control!

Cutting sugar from your diet gradually may help lessen the intensity of your symptoms, but it also means those symptoms will stick around longer. By cutting out sugar at once, your body will become used to living and functioning better without it sooner, which means a faster end to withdrawal symptoms. Do this by cutting out all forms of sugar, including those in prepackaged foods, sweetened beverages, and white flour.

Use this sugar detox as a starting point for a new and improved lifestyle. Excess sugar plays a role in obesity, but it's also been implicated in a number of chronic conditions that have serious impacts on health and quality of life. Too much sugar consumption has been linked to type 2 diabetes, heart disease, and dementia. In one study, researchers discovered that sugar actually fueled the growth of cancer cells. EEEEEKKKK, I told you "Sugar is the Devil".

STEP 1: DO NOT DRINK YOUR CALORIES

During this 7-Day Sugar Detox, liquids can be especially challenging for some and very dangerous. So much of what we drink has sugar in it so monitoring your beverages (including all alcohol - yes this includes WINE too) is going to be really key! Plus, you don't want to ruin your weight loss goals with liquids that won't even leave you feeling full or satisfied. (The only exception is my #SexyMommaShakes, which is a meal on its own.) You can find out more into at www.GlitterU.com on the healthy shakes.

Avoid all juice, alcohol, flavored teas, kombucha (just while on the detox), and any other fluids that have added ingredients. Don't worry, I'm going to hook you up with a few liquid recipe options later on in this guide.

STEP 2: THE SUGAR PURGE

Out with the Old: We have to set you up for success by cleaning out your cabinets and fridge. When the cravings hit, it's super hard to stay strong if you don't know you've got candy, cake and cookies hanging out in the kitchen somewhere. Go through your food and toss out anything that's not going to help you on your way to your sweetest life. Here are the things you should ditch:

- Processed foods, especially those with added sugars (remember to read the labels and look for words ending in "--ose").
- Sugar substitutes. I know you might think that Splenda is your friend during your detox, but honestly, it's just going to set you back. In order to really detox, you need to kick sugar and the habits associated with it.
- Grains. Say goodbye to grains! Bye bread and crackers, ouch! Remember, your body converts starch to sugar, so say bye for a little while.
- Anything with MSG.
- Anything with unhealthy fats. Check labels for trans fats and hydrogenated fats.

STEP 3: THE GOOD FATS - THEY ARE YOUR FRIEND!

If you are doing this 7-Day Sugar Detox to lose weight, you might think you should steer clear of fat too....NOPE! Healthy fat is actually a really good thing when you are trying to make diet changes. Not only does it help you feel full longer, it also shrinks your cravings and keeps your blood sugar and insulin levels balanced.

You might be wondering what is a healthy fat? Here are some of my favorites:

Avocado	Nuts
Nut butters (hello Almond Butter my BFF)	Seeds
Avocado oil	Coconut oil
Fish	

STEP 4: THE POWER OF PROTEIN

We are not here to just scale back on everything we are eating. I know right, take a breath, hew! I know that when you are making changes to your habits and diet, it's easy to just scale back on everything and sorta deprive yourself. That's not what we are going to do here....specially breakfast. Make sure you are getting enough protein. Serving sizes of protein for easy reference should always be about the size of the palm of your hand. These oh so very important proteins will balance your blood sugar and curb your cravings.

It is very important to keep in mind, just like the fats, you want to pick healthy proteins. Plant-based proteins are especially good for you! Lentils, chickpeas, quinoa, and nuts are perfect options. If you prefer to go the traditional protein route, choose fish, chicken, lean grass fed meats and eggs.

STEP 5: VEGGIES, VEGGIES AND MORE VEGGIES

Always remember WATER first, VEGGIES most! Great rule of thumb to live by. Fill up that plate and make it colorful with all the veggies. Try some new ones, your taste buds change as you age so you may have skipped some things when you were younger that you might actually love today. If you are not usually a big veggie eater, this is an awesome time to do some sampling at your local farmers' market or in the produce section of your fresh grocery store. You might just find out that you love eggplant or brussels sprouts!

Not all veggies are created equal, though. During your detox, limit potatoes (too much starch remember?), corn and carrots. Instead, try some of my personal favorites: spinach & artichoke or even asparagus if cooked right.

STEP 6: REALLY DIAL IN, FOCUS AND BE PREPARED!

If you think sugar detoxing is gonna be hard, you are correct my friend. It's not unlike quitting smoking or anything else that is addictive. Be ready! Just know that the moments of major cravings, mood swings, and hunger are unavoidable. But you don't have to be weak to them. Know that you are stronger than any craving or weakness. You can do this! Remember why you bought this book!

Being prepared can help you coast through all the ups and downs of this mini-journey (or lifelong).

How do you get prepared? The key is actually the fun part, SNACKS! Stash them in your purse, your gym bag, your car glove compartment and anywhere else you can think of. Having snacks ready to grab whenever a craving strikes can help you stay strong. I've got a secret snack recipe ideas for you in this guide too.

STEP 7: ALL THE DEETS (DETAILS): #SUGARDETOX7

Over the next 7+ days (or more!), your main focus will be to avoid all sugars that are making your life difficult in all areas including weight loss and energy. In order to do that, you need a solid plan! The next few pages, you're going to find all of my favorite tricks and recipes that are easy and NO-SUGAR! For each meal, just pick any of the listed recipes. You may or may not be eating some of the same things over and over but remember food is fuel for our bodies! This is not meant to be a buffet...it's meant to detox your system from all the bad health sugars and this is how it's done. It's still going to be delicious and it's super simple as long as you are prepared and intentional, YOU CANNOT FAIL. This doesn't have to be complicated at all.

I recommend following this guide for at least 7 days. If you feel super addicted to sugar, you can repeat this plan for as many weeks as you need. If you need additional variety, please reach out to me for other options and resources at www.GlitterU.com or www.SugarDetox7. com. Oh and don't forget to post on social media with updates from your 7-Day Sugar Detox journey so I can follow you and give you a huge shout out for your hard work! Use the hashtag #SugarDetox7 !

HERE'S YOUR SUGAR DETOX PLAN + RECIPES

Let's SLAY this Sugar!

BUILD YOUR DAILY PLAN

Remember: you want a healthy protein, fat and green at every meal.
Pick your meals and snack and get planning in your calender.

	MEAL 1	MEAL 2	MEAL 3
MONDAY			
TUESDAY			
WEDNESDAY			
THURSDAY			
FRIDAY			
SATURDAY			
SUNDAY			

Water is your best friend throughout this detox and in your everyday life. I wasn't always a fan of water, trust me. It was a choice after learning why we need it to function properly and live right that I made the conscious decision that I can drink water. Those who say, "I can't drink water", are making a choice not to drink water. It's a decision. For the sake of this 7-Day Sugar Detox, it is vital to your success. You should be drinking (minimum) ½ your body weight in ounces per day. Example: If you weigh 200 pounds, you should be consuming 100 ounces of water every single day just to have the correct brain function.

—— BEVERAGE DETOX OPTIONS ——

Water is your best friend.
Water helps you stay hydrated and flushes out toxins from your body.
Other SD (www.SugarDetox7.com) approved Sugar Detox drinks
include unsweetened green tea and herbal teas.

Drinks with zero sugar added are fine as long as they don't contain sugar substitutes.
Remember even though they might not have calories, those can keep the
sugar cravings thriving so avoid them during your detox SLAY!

TAKE THE HYDRATION TEST:

Pinch the skin on the back of your hand and let go. If your skin stays puckered for any length of time then you are more than likely dehydrated. Also, keep an eye on your urine. If the color is slightly yellow or darker, your body is telling you that it needs fluid. And since water is the safest fluid, I suggest sticking to drinking JUST WATER. Drink until your urine is consistently clear or just slightly yellow. Then you'll know your body's hydration is primed for fat loss! Write your FINDINGS BELOW:

_____

_____

_____

_____

_____

_____

_____

Water recipe option 1:

1 wedge of lemon
1 wedge of fresh ginger
Sprinkle of cayenne pepper

Drink a glass every morning
1st thing

Shred Water Recipe option 2:

Full pitcher of iced water
One cucumber cut into slices
Small grapefruit cut into wedges
Fresh mint

This keeps you fuller longer and
helps curb our appetite

WATER OPTION A
7DSD

ADD SOME FIZZ

Add some fizz. Drinking bubbly mineral water and seltzer water are great options for those who want something carbonated. Add a squeeze of lemon or lime juice for an extra kick.

WATER OPTION B
7DSD

ICE COLD

Drink it cold with a straw. Ice and a straw (make it a fun one!) can make a huge difference. I know it sounds simple, but crisp, cold water is much more enjoyable. Using a straw allows you to drink more water with ease.

WATER OPTION C
7DSD

LEMON, LIME & CUCUMBER

(add fresh lemon, lime and cucumber). Fill a pitcher with water, ice, and slice of lemon, lime and/or cucumber and stir. You now have refreshing spa-like beverage to enjoy throughout your day. This citrus and cucumber-infused water is hydrating, refreshing, and tastier than plain water.

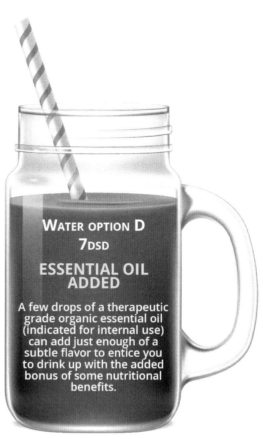

WATER OPTION D
7DSD

ESSENTIAL OIL ADDED

A few drops of a therapeutic grade organic essential oil (indicated for internal use) can add just enough of a subtle flavor to entice you to drink up with the added bonus of some nutritional benefits.

WATER OPTION
7DSD

DETOX SMOOTHIE

1 cup frozen cauliflower
1 cup spinach
1 cup coconut milk
1 scoop vanilla
super foods powder
1/2 avocado or 1 tablespoon
raw almond butter

Throw it all in a blender until well mixed. Top with chia seeds for a little extra fiber/protein boost.

FULL GROCERY LIST

APPROVED. IF IT'S NOT ON THE LIST, WE DON'T EAT IT!

GROCERY LIST: THINGS YOU CAN HAVE

Bubbly waters (carbonated)
Grapefruit
Fresh mint
Flat waters
Lemons
Limes
Cucumbers
Frozen cauliflower rice
Coconut milk
Vanilla super-foods powder (shakeo)
Avocado
Almond butter
Chia seeds
Flaxseed
Organic eggs
Spinach
Protein powder (no sugar)
Almond milk
Nut butter
Cinnamon
Black beans
Greek plain yogurt
Cashew butter
Frozen berries (all berries are allowed)

Celery
Honey crisp apples
Cacao butter
Collagen powder
Hemp seeds
Walnuts
Cashews
Almonds
Pistachios
Plain hummus
Assorted green veggies
Sweet potatoes
Chicken breasts
Coconut oil - unrefined
Romaine lettuce or butter lettuce
Roasted low sodium turkey breast
Quinoa
Yellow onion
Yellow peppers (any peppers are good)
Pumpkin seeds (unsalted preferred)
Sunflower seeds (unsalted preferred)
Mixed greens (spring mix)
Extra virgin olive oil

Vinegar
Lemon juice
Extra lean ground turkey
Lettuce - your choice, i like butter lettuce for wraps or romaine but any lettuce is fine!
Feta cheese
Pesto
Parmesan cheese
Grain free tortillas
Shredded grass fed cheese
Cumin
Paprika
Cilantro
Salmon
Asparagus
Hot sauce (crystal)
Mustard
Annie's organic horseradish mustard

SD7 BREAKFAST OPTIONS

MY GO TO

2 whole eggs

3 egg whites

1 cup steamed spinach1/4 avocado

Cook the eggs any style and enjoy with spinach and 1/4 avocado.

BREAKFAST SMOOTHIE

1 scoop no sugar added protein powder

1 cup almond milk

1 cup ice

1 tbsp nut butter

1 cup spinach

1 pinch cinnamon

Blend everything together and enjoy!

BURRITO BOWL

1 whole egg

4 egg whites

1/2 cup cauliflower rice

1/4 cup black beans

1 cup steamed spinach

1/4 avocado

1 tbsp greek yogurt

Cook the eggs any style.
Top cooked cauliflower rice, black beans and spinach with eggs.
Add avocado, salsa and additional toppings.

CHIA PUDDING

1 cup unsweetened almond milk
3- tbsp chia seeds
1 tbsp cashew or almond butter

Combine liquid and seeds together in a mason jar.
Shake well until mixed and place in the fridge overnight. Top with nut butter and enjoy!

BERRY SMOOTHIE

1 scoop protein
1 cup almond milk
1 tbsp nut butter
½ cup frozen berries

Blend everything together and enjoy!

BACK TO BASICS

2 tbsp nut butter

2 celery sticks or 1 small honey crisp apple sliced
Just like when you were a kid

ENERGY BOMBS

1 cup almond butter
¼ cup cacoa butter
¼ cup collagen powder (www.GlitterU.com for my fav)
¼ cup chia seeds and/or hemp seeds

Combine almond butter, cacao butter and collagen in a small saucepan
over medium heat. Stir until everything is smooth. Place about 1 tbsp of mixture
into small muffin tins and top with seeds. Place in freezer to harden for at least 2 hours.
1-2 is the serving size for your snack.

DELISH BERRY SNACK

1 cup almond milk
1 cup berries
½ cup ice
2 tbsp raw nut butter of choice
1 scoop protein

Blend almond milk, ice, nut butter and
protein together - that simple!

GO NUTS!

Walnuts
Cashews
Almonds
Pistachios

Mix equal parts of the above nuts together in a jar.
For your snack, enjoy ¼ cup serving!

PROTEIN SNACK FOR THE WIN!

1 hard boiled egg
2 tbsp hummus (plain)
Assortment of green veggies

Serve hard boiled egg over green veggies with
a scoop of hummus on top.

OH MY SWEET POTATO!

1 small sweet potato
1 tbsp almond butter

Poke holes in small sweet potato and cook microwave about 5 minutes or until soft all the
way through. Cut in half and drizzle with the almond butter. In a glass or shaker, mix water
and protein powder (chocolate flavored recover is my fav at www.GlitterU.com)
to sip on the side. Will fill you up and so satisfying!

ONLY GO FOR THE GREEK YOGURT!

1 cup greek yogurt plain
1 tbsp chia seeds
¼ cup blueberries
1 tbsp almond or cashew butter

In a small bowl or container, add yogurt and top with seeds and berries.

GRILLED CHICKEN AND VEGGIES

4 oz portion of grilled chicken
1 cup greens
1 small sweet potato, cubed
1 tbsp coconut oil

On a baking sheet combine all veggies and coconut oil with your favorite no sugar seasonings. Garlic, onion, sweet potato and asparagus are delicious….Bake at about 425 degrees for approx 15 minutes. Add to a bowl and top with grilled chicken.

TURKEY LETTUCE WRAPS

Large romaine lettuce leave for wrapping
4 oz portion of roasted low sodium turkey
1 tbsp hummus plain
½ small avocado

Top 2 large leaves of lettuce each with about 2 oz of roasted turkey. ½ tbsp of hummus and ¼ of the avocado. You can also add hot sauce or sriracha.

MEXICAN QUINOA IN A JAR

½ cup cooked quinoa
4 oz chicken breast
¼ grilled yellow onion
½ cup black beans
1 yellow pepper cut
½ ripe avocado

Cook quinoa according to instructions. Season chicken as desired. You could use pepper, paprika, lemon juice and garlic to start. Grill chicken approx 5-7 minutes each side. Cut and saute' onion and peppers. In a mason jar, mix quinoa, chopped chicken breast, grilled onions and peppers, and black beans. Top with avocado and your favorite salsa.

SALAD FOR THE BUSY WOMAN: ON THE GO!

4 oz portion grilled chicken chopped

2 cups mixed greens

2 tbsp pumpkin seeds

1-2 tbsp olive oil, vinegar, and ½ lemon juice for dressing

Fill a large bowl with mixed greens and top with seeds, chicken and dressing.

TURKEY BURGER

4 oz fist sized portion extra lean ground turkey

4 large lettuce leaves chopped

½ small avocado

1tbsp feta cheese

1 tbsp greek yogurt plain

Season the ground turkey with your favorite seasonings and cook over medium high for about 6 minutes on each side. Place burger on a bed of lettuce and top with remaining ingredients. You can add black beans if you like. Yum!

PROTEIN BOWL: ZEST OF PESTO!

4 oz portion grilled chicken breast

1 cup mixed roasted veggies

1 tbsp pesto

1 tbsp parmesan cheese (optional)

1 tbsp coconut oil

On a baking sheet combine all the veggies and coconut oil with your favorite no sugar added seasonings. Bake at about 425 degrees for approx 15 minutes. Add to a bowl and top with grilled chicken, pesto and cheese.

CHICKEN QUESADILLA - GRAIN FREE

4 oz. grilled chicken, chopped or shredded
2 grain free tortillas (siete' brand is the best)
⅛ cup shredded grass fed cheese
¼ tsp ground cumin
¼ tsp ground paprika
1 tbsp minced cilantro
¼ avocado
1 tbsp greek yogurt plain

Combine the cheese and grilled chicken on one tortilla. Sprinkle with cumin, cilantro and paprika. Place the second tortilla on top and cook in a pan on the stove over medium heat. Top with greek yogurt, avocado and salsa.

BAKED SALMON

4 oz salmon
½ cup cauliflower "rice"
6 asparagus spears

Preheat oven to 400. Season salmon to your liking and place skinside up in a baking pan. Place asparagus on a separate baking sheet and put both the salmon and asparagus in the oven to bake for about 15-20 minutes. Cook the cauliflower rice with fish and side of asparagus.

—————— CONGRATULATIONS! ——————

You seriously pushed through and I'm so very proud of you! You should be proud of yourself and your choices. Sugar is the Devil and it's very hard to shake it. How does it feel to be on the other side? It's time to celebrate, but NOT with sugar! It might actually make you sick at this point. It might taste horrible and feel TOXIC to your cleaned out system, because it IS! After even one week of no sugar, even a little bite of a devil cookie might taste super super sweet! And even ICKY!

As you celebrate, let it be with a new pair of tennis shoes or new yoga pants. You don't want to destroy all of your hard work with celebrating the way most of America does, with sweets - BLAH! Sugar is just as addictive now as it was before you started. Stay strong and don't slip back into your old habits.

I'm your biggest cheerleader and don't forget to get in touch with me at HeatherNewmanFitness@gmail.com to give my you testimonials. Tag me in your hashtags #SugarDetox7 and let's keep in touch, I've got so much more to share with you. Keep on pushing through, stay stocked with the right type of snacks, keep checking those sneaky labels, and you'll be able to keep enjoying your boosted natural energy, slimmer body, less bloat, less inflammation and sugar free life! Don't forget to subscribe to my blog and website so you don't miss my next release of my upcoming book too at www.GlitterU.com !

Not feeling amazing quite yet? You might need another week of the detox. Repeat this plan for another week and see how you are feeling.

This 7-Day Sugar Detox will always be here for you to refer back to, take notes in and revamp as you see fit for your life and healthy style. You've got this and I'm so stinkin' proud of you.

You did amazing I'm sure and you have just kicked one of the hardest most addictive things in the world. You heard that? The world!! You my friend are a total rockstar! Go out there, you can do anything! So proud of you!

#SugarDetox7 & www.SugarDetox7.com

Congratulations! I am so proud of you!
XX, Heather

TESTIMONIALS

"Everyone knows the path to sustained health and nutrition is a lifestyle change. However, most of us need a little something to jumpstart the change. This is it! It's a strict prescriptive guide (with taste choices) that explains why and how to kick the sugar cravings. After seven days I discovered the sugar cravings subsided, I was a few pounds lighter and ready for that lifestyle change. Going from strict to healthy was easy. A colleague commented 'you always seem to be snacking on a piece of fruit or veggies.' I guess my sugar snacking was noticeably to others." Diane Boyle

"First I should start by saying I have been on a health journey for 6 months. I started with clean eating, portion control and a daily exercise program. For me, participating in the Sugar detox program was a no brainer. I "thought" this would be a simple challenge. I wasn't a candy eater, I don't drink soft drinks, and I limit myself to coffee once a week. Apparently I was wrong. This program is an amazing way to cleanse your body. It is very clean eating. I experienced several of the side effects discussed in the book around day 3 and 4. Fatigue and headache. I enjoyed the detox water. I chose the grapefruit, cucumber and mint recipe. A nice thing was that my kids enjoyed the water also, and asked for me to continue making with one modification. Overall, I lost 2 lbs and 3 1/2 inches. I would recommend this detox to anyone."
Roxann Davis

"I absolutely found this guide and detox plan so easy to follow, it was so step by step. I bought the groceries on the list, drank my detox water everyday, all day..& planned my meals according to the foods that were accepted. I was full most of the time, I learned so many alternative foods and snacks i can now eat instead of bad choices I may have chosen before. Foods I actually love. I lost 6 pounds in 7 days!! That's amazing to me!! I will use this guide over and over for all of my future occasions,..weddings, anniversaries, trips, Birthdays, or just to feel better for myself. I cannot day enough about this guide!! THANK YOU THANK YOU THANK YOU!! I give this book 5stars!! ✩✩✩✩✩& 2thumbs up!!" Diane Favalora

"I am very happy that I chose to try the 7 day sugar detox! I thought I was a pretty healthy eater, but this plan forced me to take a closer look at the foods that I eat. I realized I was eating a lot more sugar than I realized. The Sugar is the Devil 7-Day Sugar Detox plan was easy to follow with great tips and recipes. My favorite was the grapefruit, mint & cucumber detox water which will remain a staple in my house from now on. Some of the key benefits that I noticed were feeling full longer, less mental fog, more energy, and decreased joint pain upon wakening. I recommend this plan to anyone and everyone because you will feel better and you will become better educated about your food choices!" Heather Seaner

On June 3,2019, I began a journey to a healthier me. I have been very hesitant to share as I have been on this journey many times before and for whatever reason didn't stick to it and reverted back to old ways. This time is different or so I hope. At the beginning of my journey, I had decided that enough was enough; I was responsible for my life and I needed to take control of it. I started by watching what I ate, limiting carbs and sugar, and committing to go to the gym (a place I've dreaded). I had been a member at this gym in the past, but given situations with and home life, had to switch gyms to accommodate having a child. I only sporadically went to the gym during the past year (when I was trying to get back on track) and prior to that I haven't frequented a gym since getting on the fertility journey over 3-4 years ago. I finally decided to make this commitment to MYSEF. Some things changed with work so I was able to go back to my original gym. I like doing group fitness classes so having never tried it before, I decided to try Barre. This is where I met Heather Newman. My first class, I was nervous, but she made me feel so comfortable and welcomed the entire time. After class, she sat with me for 45 minutes asking me various questions about myself and my goals. I was immediately inspired by her and found her to be extremely motivational. She also invited me to follow her pages on Facebook. All of this leads me to where i am today now.

Heather shared her "7-DAy Detox Guide: Sugar is the Devil" on her page and my interest was piqued since I've always loved SWEETS! I decided to be a part of her small beta test group. I won't say the detox was easy, but definitely doable and so worth it! I wasn't a fan of the detox waters, I tried the grapefruit/mint/cucumber and lemon/mint/ cucumber. The grocery list is a little intimidating at first because it appears so limited; however, you can mix things up and create variety. I still ate a lot of the same meals because it was easier to make more so it would last longer since I'm not a fan of cooking. I loved having the eggs with spinach, parmesan cheese, avocado, and hot sauce for breakfast so I ate it every day and plan to continue to eat it often. Some of the things I tried, I wasn't a huge fan of, but overall, the food was satisfying. I did have a few things not on the list; however, I made healthier choices than I would have previously and NOT have sugar! I did struggle with a headache the first few days, but I also had allergies going on so it could have been a combination of the two things. I also only exercised 3 or 4 of the days. I lost a total of 3 inches and 10 pounds in the 7 days. Ultimately, this plan has helped me be more conscience of the things I'm putting into my body and also how important it is you READ food labels to see what's actually in the things we eat. I feel so much better after completing the 7 day; my energy has increased, the craving subsided. I lost water weight and feel less bloated. I plan to continue limiting the sugar and artificial sweeteners, etc.; however, I definitely believe in occasional treats. I also want to incorporate different food and encouragement when I needed it most! So thankful to have met this awesome woman. She has taught me so much in this short time; most importantly that if I get off track, don't get stuck there, just move on and get back on track.

As of now, I have lost a total of 43 pounds and gained so much in other aspects! I hope to continue my journey and adapt it to my everyday life for the rest of my life."

Rebecca LeBlanc

"First of all, I feel like I've been on a diet my entire life. I have never done a detox, especially a sugar detox, I am a chocoholic, so I thought it would be a tough challenge, but I was certainly up for it. I had done well on Atkins but that has such a broad range of recipes and foods to eat. The limiting of foods when I saw the menus was a shock to me but I thought I could do this. I have suffered with IBS for over 38 years, and I am on several medications. I have to be careful what I eat and drink. So, the only detox water I drank was lemon lime and cucumber. I was afraid the acid was going to upset my stomach but I did well. I wasn't a big egg eater but I ate plenty of scrambled eggs and spinach or spinach omelets. I also loved boiled eggs. I didn't like the taste of organic eggs. I don't know if anyone else notices the difference. I also had 1/2 avocados for my breakfasts most of the days. I was usually always on the go so this was the easiest for me. For snacks I usually had a honey crisp apple, which by the way is very sweet, it helped with sugar cravings. I had celery sticks, a handful of nuts, and protein shakes only twice because they are very filling (I wasn't very hungry). I really didn't find myself needing snacks or craving anything after lunch or dinner. I was never one to snack in between meals before, but I knew there were plenty of options, and good ones. Lunches were easy for me. I really liked having turkey wraps with hummus and avocado.

Sometimes I would add black beans, feta cheese, boiled eggs, oil and vinegar. When I am hot, I don't like eating a lot of food. The majority of my dinners included grilled chicken and turkey burgers. I had sweet potatoes, cauliflower rice and asparagus as sides. I used coconut oil and olive oil for cooking. I was so full with water that my portions were plenty enough. I didn't mind eating the same thing each day even though you offered many more menu options. I eat what I like and what was easy for me to make. I am used to eating out every day and night so I am not one for preparing meals, so the simpler the better. I have to say the only thing I missed was my coffee first thing in the morning. I always looked forward to it. I had a few headaches the first few days and was sluggish but I did not cheat!! I followed the program and it paid off. When I started the program I took measurements and I lost an inch everywhere including my waist, hips, bust, arms, thighs, and lost a total of 7 lbs. I did this without any exercising!! I plan on continuing this program for at least 2 more weeks, maybe more. I went to see my doctor today and she looked at me and said right away " there's something different about you". I said my hair is finally growing out. No, she said "you look happy!!". I said "I am!!" I finally feel like I have accomplished something that I've wanted to do for a long time, feel healthier!! This is a terrific detox!! I feel great with so much more energy. Overall I would say this is a very simple detox for someone to follow who has never done one before. You will never be hungry, and have plenty of options to satisfy your cravings. I would recommend it to anyone who needs to jump start any weight loss and forget about the need to have sugar in their diet!! What's sugar???? Heather you have been a great coach and motivator. I am grateful for your guidance as I went through my first detox. It was a great week! SUCCESS!!" *- Pamela Clarke*

'I began the 7 day sugar detox journey on September 3, 2019. I honestly had some serious doubts as to whether I could be successful for the entire 7 days. Everyone who knows me well knows of my morning addiction to orange juice and my nightly craving for ice cream. Not to mention my intense love of pasta.

I began by reading through Heather's easy to follow 7 day detox book. Then I went to the grocery to stock up on the recommended items on her food list. Having these foods readily available at home definitely made all the difference!

There are so many healthy choice snacks, delicious smoothies and easy to follow recipes! I never felt hungry and never once craved sugar(except in my coffee)! I did have the usual symptoms of detox such as headaches and fatigue but, on the 6 1/2 and 7 th day I felt amazing! Not only physically but also mentally. I lost 3 1/2 lbs. and 1". More importantly, I proved to myself that I had more will power and self control than I thought. I have also kicked my orange juice habit and still haven't craved ice cream.

Thank you Heather for helping me prove to myself that "I can do it!"
Carolyn George

MY JOURNAL

7-DAY SUGAR DETOX METHOD:

SUGAR IS THE DEVIL
(GUIDE, PLAN AND WORKBOOK)

by HEATHER NEWMAN

There was a point in my life that I was a Diet Coke and Funyuns kind of girl! It wasn't until I had my two boys that I started to really consider what I was putting into my body and how to properly care for it. I grew up with the "eat less, count calories" mindset. UGH! I was a dancer my entire life. Once I graduated college, I became certified in group fitness and taught "step aerobic" classes 6x/week. 18 years later I rekindled my love of teaching group fitness coming back focussed on complete toning at the BARRE (less impact) with all aspects of applying balance, pilates & ballet movement at the barre including strength training with complete muscle isolation. I created and still teach #HeatherNewmanBootyBarre100 and #HeatherNewmanBootyBarre365.

I was voted "Northshore's Best Coach of the year 2018" and nominated "Ms. Health and Fitness 2019". I have trained and taught others to find and share their passion for fitness! I love teaching classes but my heart still longed to help others more than just that 1 hour I had with them during our class time. I created an opportunity to help others exponentially in addition to my classes and have loved it! I am able to help others through my true passion for fitness, nutrition, mindset & supplementation. Although I'll always be a dancer at heart, I feel my assignment is to be your biggest cheerleader in LIFE! I've created my #getUnstuck method and IT WORKS!

Let's lock arms - I'd love to work with you on your goals too.
JOIN MY COACHING TEAM: www.JoinNolaFit.com
Subscribe to my Podcast on Itunes: #getUnstuck with Heather Newman
Follow me on Facebook: Heather Newman Fitness
Follow me on Instagram: GlitterU

If you've found yourself here, reading this book and using this method, I'm sure you have been struggling with SUGAR most of your life. Being a complete chocoholic for most of my life, I am fully aware of the addiction. The scary thing is that sugar comes in so many forms, we may think we are eliminating it from our diet when in fact, we are still supporting the addiction through other food sources. I call this the sneaky "devil" sugars. They are the ones that most people aren't really clear on or aware of. It's not as cut and dry as the sugar found in candy, cake and cookies. Regardless of your sugar cravings, through whichever avenue you struggle with the most, you are in the right place and I'm so glad we are on this journey together for the next 7-days or even longer. I would truly love to hear from you once you've finished my sugar detox method. Please be sure to subscribe to my website at www.GlitterU.com and leave your testimonial from this experience at www.SugarDetox7.com. Let's get this party started! Promise me you'll try to stay nice to everyone around you while you are cleanse your mind, body and soul from the toxic sugar(s).

Made in the USA
Columbia, SC
11 February 2020

87786762R00033